BASIC SURVIVAL T1

Malcolm Bowler AKA JJR SURVIVAL

Disclaimer: The information contained within this Book is strictly for educational purposes. If you wish to apply ideas contained in this Book, you are taking full responsibility for your actions. Be sure to check all relevant laws regarding hunting and trapping in your area .

BE AWARE THAT MOST OF THE ITEMS MENTIONED WILL BE ILLEGAL TO USE UNLESS IN A REAL SURVIVAL SITUATION.

CONTENTS

This book is a compilation of the simplest traps i could think of , there are many much more complicated traps that can be made but each require time, effort and skill to make, hopefully these traps will be easy enough for even a novice to practice making .

In a survival situation trapping will be the most efficient method of getting meat . simply because once made the trap will do its work while you can do other things or even just rest .

split fork deadfall

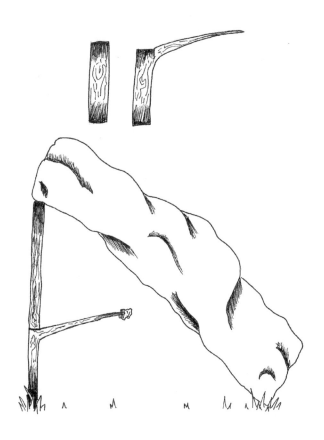

SPLIT FORK DEADFALL TRAP

This is a simple deadfall trap with a 2 piece trigger the animal attempts to take the Bait from the end of the stick and dislodges the trigger causing the deadfall weight to fall on top of the animal .

HOW TO MAKE:

STEP 1: find a tree branch / stick with a side branch sticking out, shave the side branch to point

STEP 2: the stick is cut in half just above the side branch as pictured and bait is placed on the end of the side branch

STEP 3: the 2 halves are placed together and a deadfall weight is placed on top.

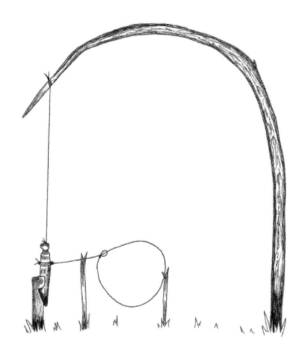

spring snare

SPRING SNARE

A snare is attached to a notched stick which has a string line running up to a bent sapling or a counterweight over a branch , the notched stick is held down in place by another notched stick pushed into the ground, 2 small sticks are used to keep the snare open , when an animal is caught in the snare the 2 notches dislodge and the snare flies up into the air and keeps the animal off the ground and away from other animals, it also keeps the animal from being able to struggle and break out of the snare

HOW TO MAKE:

STEP 1: you need snare wire , paracord, 2 small thin sticks, a sapling or weight (log/rock) and 2 sticks one long enough to be pushed into the ground to anchor the sapling down and one to attach your snare and long cord to

STEP 2; first cut a notch as pictured into the shorter stick and attach the snare and a long length of paracord ,

STEP 3: now sharpen the longer stick and cut a notch into this one too and push / hammer it into the ground , now lock the 2 notches together and attach the paracord line to a sapling or weight bending it down to make sure it will spring back up ,
STEP 4: now set your snare up using the 2 thin sticks to hold it in place
STEP 5: a small barricade of sticks can be added each side or around the back and bait added to funnel animal into the snare.

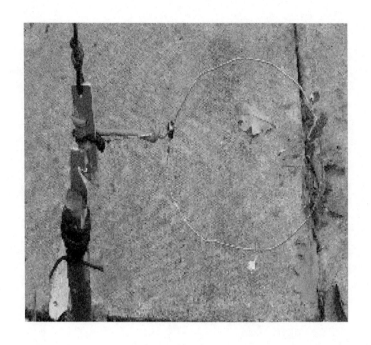

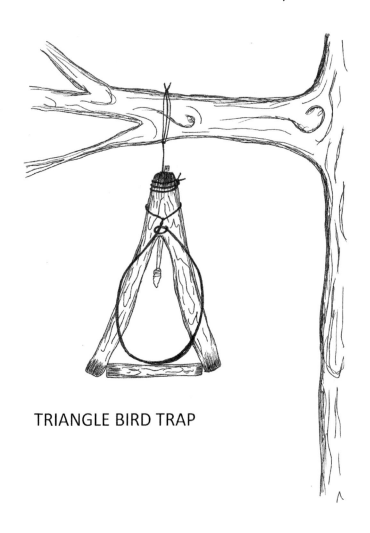

TRIANGLE BIRD TRAP

TRIANGLE BIRD TRAP / COAT HANGER TRAP

A simple trap for catching smaller birds, the bird will land on the lower section of the triangle to eat the bait , when it lands the perch will fall away and the bird will get caught in the noose

HOW TO MAKE:

STEP 1: Take a forked stick and cut it to a similar shape as shown in the picture

STEP 2: attach a light snare at the top of the fork and tie a thin stick pointing down with a long length of string the rest of the string is used to tie the trap to a tree branch

STEP 3: now a smaller stick is placed between the forks but push it into place just enough to hold it , making sure it will fall way if a bird lands on it , alternatively a snare could be placed on each side awell.

samsons post deadfall

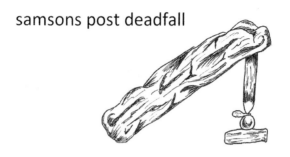

SAMSONS POST DEADFALL TRAP

A log is balanced on a 2 piece trigger consisting of an upright stick and small round (or half round) log on top of another (1 log split into 2 can also be used) the bait is placed between the 2 and 2 or more sticks are used along the side to stop the log toppling off the other one , when the animal tries to take the bait it dislodges the upright stick and brings down the log on the top

HOW TO MAKE:

STEP 1: place 1 log on the floor push some sticks in the ground along the sides

STEP 2: carve a stick with a blunt point, and place a small log or stone on the bottom log

STEP 3; now place bait on the small log / stone and put the the upright stick in place

STEP 4; now put the top log carefully on the trigger

an alternative method is to use rocks instead of logs and a round stone instead of a small log for the trigger.

wooden cage

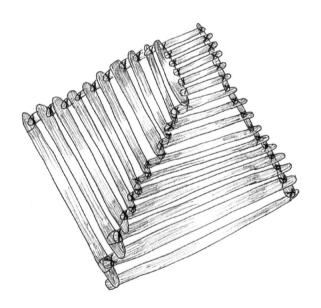

WOODEN CAGE

A pyramid cage can be made instead of using logs or rocks , to make a simple cage start off by making a square with 4 sticks tied at the corners , now add more sticks alternating them as you go and tying each one to the ones below essentially the same method as building a log cabin but each time bring the sticks inwards a bit towards the middle until you reach your desired height then add a few more on top and tie them all tightly in place , you can then use this with any of the various triggers mentioned in this book .

2 stick deadfall

2 STICK DEADFALL

A very simple trap using 2 sticks an upright stick is balanced under another stick with a deadfall weight on top of it, bait is placed between the deadfall and the stick , when the animal tries to take the bait it will dislodge the trigger and be crushed under the deadfall

HOW TO MAKE:

STEP 1: take 2 sticks one longer than the other and and tie some bait to smaller stick

STEP 2: now balance the 2 as shown making sure the upright stick is as far to the edge of the deadfall as will allow

split stick deadfall

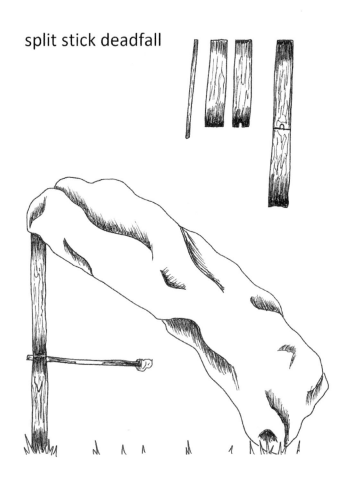

SPLIT STICK DEADFALL

A simple deadfall trap, the trigger is 2 bits of stick with a small groove carved into the top of the bottom stick and another smaller stick is placed into the groove between the 2 to act as a trigger / bait stick , an animal will push or nudge the stick and cause the 2 main sticks to come apart and the rock will fall

HOW TO MAKE:

STEP 1; Take a strong stick and cut it in 2 in the middle ,

STEP 2: now carve a small groove into the end of one stick .

STEP 3: then take a smaller stick and carve it to fit tightly into the groove ,

STEP 4: now put the 2 together with smaller stick between them and balance a large rock / log or cage on top as shown in the picture.

wooden cage

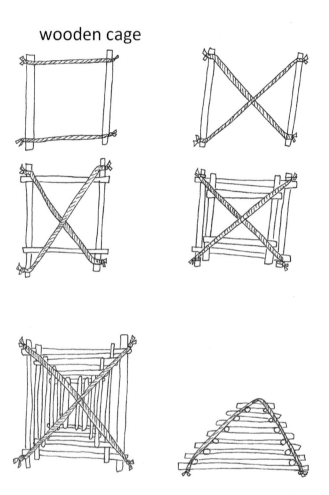

WOODEN CAGE

Another simple log cabin type cage can be made by tying 2 strings to 2 sticks as shown in the pictures starting from top left , once 2 strings are tied to the 2 sticks you then cross them over , now you simply start adding sticks alternating each side you add them and keep pushing them under the string each time as you go, the sticks you add will make the string get tighter and tighter eventually you can no longer add anymore sticks and the whole lot will be held tightly together .

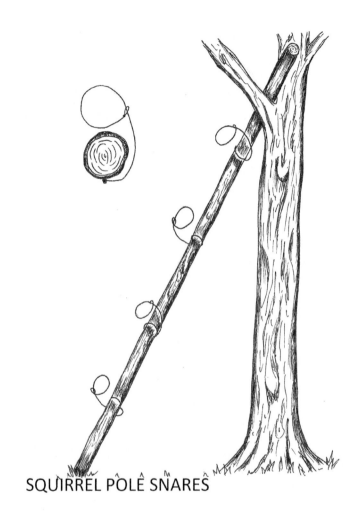

SQUIRREL POLE SNARES

SQUIRREL POLE SNARE

A squirrel pole snare is simply a set of snares set on a long wooden pole leaned against a tree , the squirrel will instinctively go up the leaning pole rather than the vertical tree and will get caught in one of the snares , the snares have to be tied so they come from under the pole , this way the squirrel feels snare around its neck and will hopefully try to jump from the pole and will be left hanging under the pole

HOW TO MAKE:

STEP 1: Take the longest pole you can find and attach as many snares as you can fit on the pole leaving about a foot and half between each snare ,have the snares attached under the pole but come round to the top , like in the picture ,

STEP 2; now place your pole against a tree where you have seen squirrels or place leaning in a fruit or nut tree.

tripwire deadfall

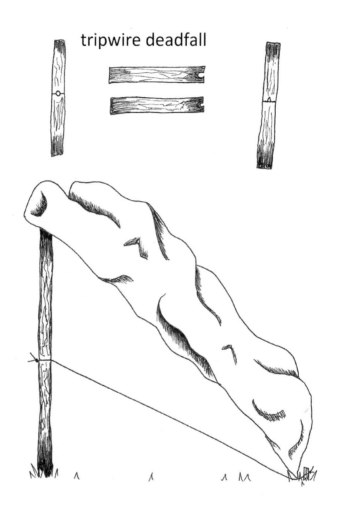

TRIPWIRE DEADFALL

A trap using 2 sticks with a string trigger ,
the string can either be through a groove in
one stick with knot at the end or tied around
one of them , the other end is tied to a small
peg at the back of the deadfall, the animal
dislodges the trigger when it steps on or
nudges the string , bait could be tied to the
string or placed at the back of the trap.

HOW TO MAKE:

STEP 1: take a stick ,cut it in half and either
carve a groove or or tie a string to the stick,

STEP 2: if you choose the groove method ,
tie a large strong knot in the end of the string

STEP 3; , now place the 2 sticks together
with the string between and laid on the floor
towards where the back of the deadfall is

STEP 4: now push a small peg into the
ground and tie the other end of the string to
this now place your deadfall on to the sticks.

cambodia bird trap

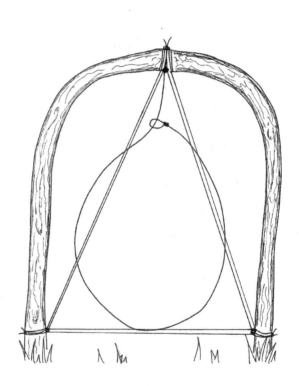

CAMBODIA BIRD TRAP

A snare is a set and held in place in the arch by doubled cords of string , the arch is pushed into the ground until it looks like the picture, it is set on a trail or a place a ground birds / water birds will pass and be caught

HOW TO MAKE:

STEP 1: take a bendy stick and bend it into an arch like in the picture , but have the arch much longer than as shown to allow it to be pushed into the ground now take a doubled / 2 long bit of string and tie it along the bottom to hold the arch together ,

STEP 2: now take your strings and tie again from the bottom to the top middle of the arch and back down again to the otherside at the bottom like in the picture,

STEP 3: tie a snare in place at the top and use the doubled strings to hold the snare in place by having a string each side of your snare

STEP 4: place your archway and snare in a place that a bird will have to pass through.

y stick deadfall trap

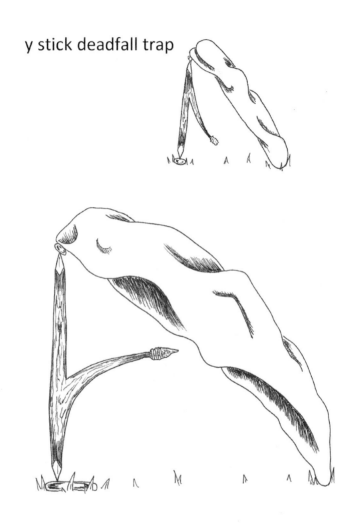

Y STICK DEADFALL TRAP

This simple deadfall trap is made using a forked stick from a branch, when the animal tries to take the bait it will dislodge the trigger and bring the deadfall down on top of it.

HOW TO MAKE:

STEP 1: find a forked stick and a deadfall weight and a few flat pebbles or bark etc

STEP 2: cut the fork as shown and to your required length and sharpen all ends of the fork points

STEP 3: add your bait before, then put a flat pebble or similar on the floor and place your trigger either way up (as shown) on the pebble

STEP 4: now balance the deadfall on the fork trigger , you can add another pebble at the top if required but have the trigger as near to edge as possible.

BIRD SNARES

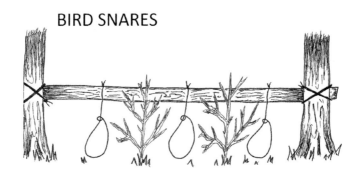

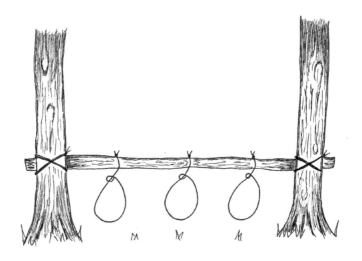

BIRD SNARES

A pole is set horizontally across a path where ground birds have been seen passing, the gaps can be filled with branches to funnel the animal through the snares, they try to pass and will be caught in the snares

HOW TO MAKE:

STEP 1: take a long pole and tie it between 2 trees or 2 posts banged into ground where ground birds have been seen passing

STEP 2: take snares and set along the pole as shown

STEP 3: fill in any areas that birds can through.

snare

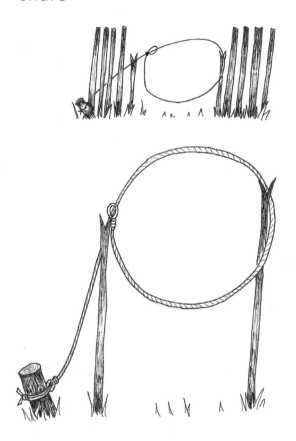

SNARE

A simple snare is made of brass or metal cable, lightweight bird snares can be made from paracord etc, the snare is attached to a peg that driven in the ground and the snare is held open with 2 small forked twigs, place the trap on an animals run,or a place where an animal is passing through.

HOW TO MAKE:

STEP 1: take a metal cable or paracord /strong string etc and make a small loop one end now pass the other end through this to make a noose

STEP 2: attach the snare to a strong peg and hammer this into the ground now take a few small twigs and place them as shown to hold the snare open, make sure everything is good and secure you will have to judge the height that your targets head will be when it is walking to get the height of your snare right and make the opening larger than the animals head too so it can pass through.

3 stick deadfall

3 STICK DEADFALL TRAP

3 balanced sticks hold a deadfall weight up, the weight is pushing onto one stick that is held back and in place by the others when an animal takes the bait it will release the other sticks and bring the deadfall down, THE TRIGGER MAY HAVE TO BE IN A MORE SLANTED POSITIOn

HOW TO MAKE :

STEP 1: take 3 sticks each roughly half the size of each other , some of your sticks may need to be cut to fit

STEP 2: place some bait on the smallest sick

STEP 3; cut a small notch as shown in the middle size stick at one end to fit the other stick into it.

Step 4: place the upright longest stick at an angle and put the middle stick in place and hold with 1 hand near the top, now place the deadfall on to the middle size stick as shown

STEP 5: place the bait stick between the 2 other sticks , make sure the longest stick is positioned so it is not under the deadfall otherwise it may get stuck..

squirrel snare

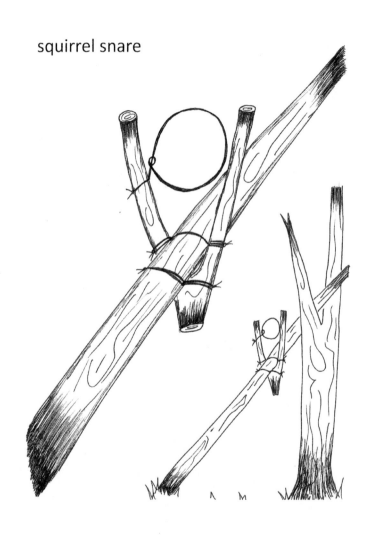

SQUIRREL SNARE

This squirrel trap is similar to the usual pole trap but with an added part to funnel the squirrel and hold the snare better, the pole is set against a tree as usual but a forked stick is cut and tied to the pole as shown , then the snare is attached to the pole or the fork ,

HOW TO MAKE:

STEP 1: find a pole that can be leaned against a suitable tree

STEP 2: find a small tree fork and cut it as shown

STEP 3: tie the fork to a branch and add the snare on one fork, the snare could also be attached to the pole incase the squirrel breaks the fork.

spring snare

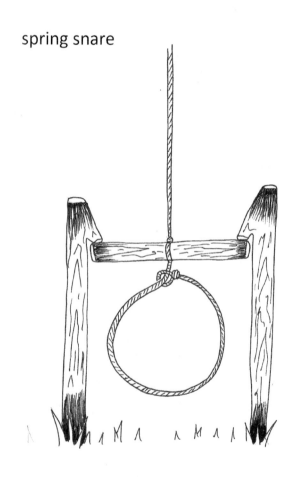

SPRING SNARE

A snare attached to a bit of wood is held in place by 2 sticks with chopped off branches that hold the stick from being lifted in the air, the other end of the snare is attached to a springy branch or weight , once the animal has been caught in the snare it will pull loose the stick being held down and it will be raised into the air

HOW TO MAKE:

STEP 1: get 2 sticks with side branches and cut these short like in the picture and hammer these into the ground

STEP 2: now a take a stick that will fit between the 2 and add a snare and a long cord to it ,

STEP 3: the other end of the long cord attach this to a weight over a branch or to a bendy sapling.

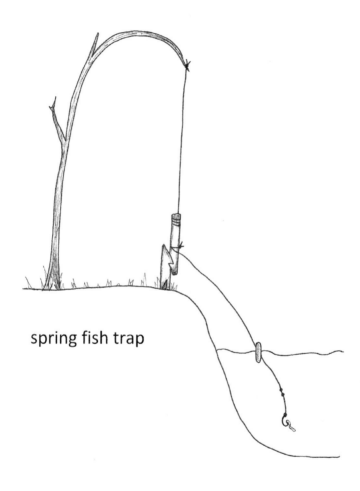

spring fish trap

SPRING FISH TRAP

The spring fish is essentially a spring snare but with a fishing hook setup rather an a snare , when the fish takes the bait and pulls it dislodges the the 2 notched sticks and the sapling flies up into the air as does the line which should set the hook in to the fishes mouth

HOW TO MAKE:

STEP 1: find a bendy sapling or a branch that a line of string can be thrown over and counter weight attach attached

STEP 2: carve 2 sticks the same as a spring snare and hammer one into the ground as your anchor

STEP 3; attach your fishing line and whatever weights ,floats ,bait , hooks etc and bend the sapling down and attach the notched sticks together and put the end with hook into the water .

Many thanks for reading my book ,
if you are interested check out my youtube
channel: JJR SURVIVAL
3/2/18